BOSTON TERRIERS

by Allan Morey

Consultant: Jennifer Zablotny
Doctor of Veterinary Medicine
American Veterinary
Medical Association

Pebble®
Plus

CAPSTONE PRESS
a capstone imprint

Pebble Plus is published by Capstone Press,
1710 Roe Crest Drive, North Mankato, Minnesota 56003
www.mycapstone.com

Library of Congress Cataloging-in-Publication Data is available on the Library of Congress website.

ISBN 978-1-5157- 1963-2 (hardcover)
ISBN 978-1-5157-1969-4 (eBook PDF)

Summary: Simple text and full-color photographs describe Boston terriers.

Editorial Credits
Emily Raij, editor; Juliette Peters, designer;
Pam Mitsakos, media researcher; Laura Manthe, production specialist

Photo Credits
Alamy: Big Cheese Photo LLC, 17; Getty Images: Mark Raycroft/Minden Pictures, 4-5; iStockphoto:
Beverley Vycital, 21; Shutterstock: C_Gara, 12–13, Clement Morin, 11, Eric Isselee, cover, Gary
Boisvert, 1, kostolom3000, 3, back cover top left, Tasha Karidis, 19, Victoria Rak, 15, vlastas, design
element throughout book; SuperStock: Jean Michel Labat /ardea.com/Pantheon, 7; Thinkstock:
ArmanWerthPhotography, 9

Note to Parents and Teachers

The Tiny Dogs set supports national science standards related to life science. This book describes
and illustrates Boston terriers. The images support early readers in understanding the text. The
repetition of words and phrases helps early readers learn new words. This book also introduces
early readers to subject-specific vocabulary words, which are defined in the Glossary section. Early
readers may need assistance to read some words and to use the Table of Contents, Glossary, Read
More, Internet Sites, Critical Thinking Using the Common Core, and Index sections of the book.

Printed in the United States of America.
009656F16

TABLE OF CONTENTS

Fun and Playful 4

Snorts and Grunts 8

Boston Terriers as Pets 16

Glossary 22

Read More 23

Internet Sites 23

Critical Thinking
    Using the Common Core 24

Index 24

FUN AND PLAYFUL

Do you like small, playful dogs?
Then you might like Boston
terriers. People call them BTs
for short.

Boston terriers were bred in the
late 1800s to fight other dogs.
Now they make loving family pets.

SNORTS AND GRUNTS

Boston terriers are small dogs. They stand about as tall as a bowling pin. They weigh no more than 25 pounds (11 kilograms).

Boston terriers have short coats. Their fur is white with at least one other color. This can be black or red-black. Some have a mix of light and dark colors called brindle.

Boston terriers do not bark much.
But they can still be noisy.
Their short muzzles make them
snort and grunt. They snore too!

Very cold or hot weather is hard
for Boston terriers. Their short
coats do not keep them warm.
Their short muzzles make it hard
to pant and cool down.

BOSTON TERRIERS AS PETS

Boston terriers make great family pets. They enjoy being around people. They are good with kids. Boston terriers also get along well with other animals.

These smart dogs are easy
to train. They want to please
their owners. Many Boston terriers
enjoy playing fetch.

It is easy to care for
Boston terriers. They need little
grooming. A short walk each day
is enough exercise. Healthy Boston
terriers can live up to 14 years.

GLOSSARY

breed—to mate and produce young

brindle—a coat pattern with specks and streaks of light and dark markings

coat—an animal's hair or fur

exercise—a physical activity done in order to stay healthy and fit

fetch—to go after something and bring it back

groom—to clean and make an animal look neat

muzzle—an animal's nose, mouth, and jaws

pant—to breathe quickly with an open mouth; some animals pant to cool off

terrier—a type of small dog originally used for hunting

train—to prepare for something by learning or practicing new skills

READ MORE

Brett, Flora. *A Dog's View of the World.* Pet Perspectives. North Mankato, Minn.: Capstone Press, 2016.

Carr, Aaron. *Dogs.* Science Kids: Life Cycles. New York: AV2 by Weigl, 2016.

Landau, Elaine. *Boston Terriers Are the Best!* Best Dogs Ever. Minneapolis: Lerner, 2011.

INTERNET SITES

FactHound offers a safe, fun way to find Internet sites related to this book. All of the sites on FactHound have been researched by our staff.

Here's all you do:

Visit *www.facthound.com*

Type in this code: 9781515719632

 Check out projects, games and lots more at
www.capstonekids.com

CRITICAL THINKING USING THE COMMON CORE

1. Would you like to have a Boston terrier for a pet? What traits do you like about Boston terriers? (Integration of Knowledge and Ideas)

2. Why is it hard for a Boston terrier to handle very hot or cold weather? (Key Ideas and Details)

INDEX

breeding, 6
coats, 10, 14
colors, 10
exercise, 20
grooming, 20
height, 8
life span, 20

muzzles, 12, 14
noises, 12
pets, 6, 16
training, 18
weight, 8